NASCAR
RACING

By Dustin Long

SportsZone

An Imprint of Abdo Publishing
www.abdopublishing.com

www.abdopublishing.com

Published by Abdo Publishing, a division of ABDO, PO Box 398166, Minneapolis, Minnesota 55439. Copyright © 2015 by Abdo Consulting Group, Inc. International copyrights reserved in all countries. No part of this book may be reproduced in any form without written permission from the publisher. SportsZone™ is a trademark and logo of Abdo Publishing.

Printed in the United States of America, North Mankato, Minnesota
042014
092014

THIS BOOK CONTAINS
RECYCLED MATERIALS

Cover Photo: Jae C. Hong/AP Images
Interior Photos: Jae C. Hong/AP Images, 1; Bill Friel/AP Images, 4–5, Steve Helber/AP Images, 7; Action Sports Photography/Shutterstock Images, 9, 36; Christopher Halloran/Shutterstock Images, 11; Pete Wright/AP Images, 12–13; Faireleth/AP Images, 14; Ric Feld/AP Images, 17; Photo Works/Shutterstock Images, 18; AP Images, 20–21, 23; Harold Valentine/AP Images, 25; John Raoux/AP Images, 27; Beelde Photography/Shutterstock Images, 28–29, 44; Peter Cosgrove/AP Images, 30–31; NKP, Nigel Kinrade/AP Images, 33; David Duprey/AP Images, 35; Lynne Sladky/AP Images, 38–39; Chris O'Meara/AP Images, 41; GB/AP Images, 42

Editor: Patrick Donnelly
Series Designer: Craig Hinton

Library of Congress Control Number: 2014932879

Cataloging-in-Publication Data
Long, Dustin.
 NASCAR racing / Dustin Long.
  p. cm. -- (Inside the speedway)
Includes bibliographical references and index.
ISBN 978-1-62403-406-0
1. Automobile racing--Juvenile literature. 2. Stock car racing--Juvenile literature. 3. NASCAR (Association)--Juvenile literature. I. Title.
796.72--dc23

                                                    2014932879

TABLE OF CONTENTS

1 Crazy Crashes,
Dynamite Drivers 5

2 Racing's Roots Run Deep 13

3 Stock Cars to Magnificent
Machines 21

4 Super Skills 31

5 The King and His Court 39

Glossary 46

For More Information 47

Index 48

About the Author 48

chapter 1

CRAZY CRASHES, DYNAMITE DRIVERS

The destroyed stock car was on fire. Driver Juan Pablo Montoya limped away from the wreck. The TV announcers were confused by the scene.

"Holy cow! What happened?" NASCAR analyst Darrell Waltrip asked on TV.

The 2012 Daytona 500 was already under caution. That meant the race cars

A fiery crash knocked Juan Pablo Montoya out of the 2012 Daytona 500.

circled the track at Daytona International Speedway at 70 miles per hour (mph), or 113 kilometers per hour (km/h), instead of 200 mph (322 km/h). They slowed because safety trucks and jet dryers were on the track. Those trucks used jet engines to clean the racing surface.

Montoya had crashed into a jet dryer. Spilled fuel caught fire. Flames stretched across the track. Firemen arrived. The race was delayed more than two hours.

"It's the most bizarre thing I've ever seen," Waltrip said on the broadcast.

NASCAR's history features many wild crashes. The sport's first season was in 1949. A car rolled over in the first race. In the years since, many cars have flown off the track and flipped several times. But there had never been a wreck like Montoya's.

There is more to NASCAR's history than crashes. The sport also is known for its excellent drivers and close races.

NASCAR driver Kyle Busch shows off the safety harness that protects drivers in case of crashes.

That has helped NASCAR become one of the most popular sports in the United States. Fans enjoy watching the cars bang into each other. Fans also enjoy watching their favorite drivers race around the tracks.

NASCAR has grown through the years. Drivers used to race on dirt tracks. Their vehicles were called stock cars and looked just like cars found on the road. Some even drove their race cars to the track in the early days. Now, the cars are built in race shops where as many as 500 people work on them. The cars race on paved tracks. Some tracks hold more than twice as many people as the largest football stadiums.

NASCAR races used to be held mainly in the southern United States. In 2014 the NASCAR Sprint Cup Series held races in 20 states. Races are held as far west as California and as far north as New Hampshire. Drivers race on many different tracks. They race on road courses where they make left and right turns. They race on short tracks, which are less than 1 mile (1.6 km) long. They also race on tracks more than 2 miles (3.2 km) in length.

The sport's most famous race remains the Daytona 500. It is

Safety First

Racing remains dangerous, but protection for drivers continues to improve. Drivers must wear helmets to protect their heads in crashes. Their uniforms protect drivers in fires. Drivers are held in their seats by special safety harnesses. The cars are also designed to protect the drivers. All these improvements have helped many NASCAR drivers walk away from crashes. However, safety equipment is not perfect. Dale Earnhardt Sr. died in a crash at the 2001 Daytona 500. That led to increased safety measures for all drivers.

The Daytona 500 is the biggest race on the NASCAR schedule.

held at the track in Daytona Beach, Florida. The first Daytona 500 was held in 1959. Jimmie Johnson won it in 2013. He and his team collected more than $1.5 million for that win.

But the NASCAR Sprint Cup Series is about more than one race. The season is divided into two parts. The first 26 races determine who qualifies for the season championship. Those drivers race for the title in the final 10 races.

Richard Petty and Dale Earnhardt Sr. are the only drivers to have won seven season championships through 2013.

But Johnson won his sixth title in 2013. Petty won 200 races, more than any other driver. That is one of the reasons why he is still known as "The King."

Petty's last victory was among the most memorable in the sport's history. He won on July 4, 1984, at Daytona. What made it special was that President Ronald Reagan attended the race. It was the first time a US president had been to a NASCAR race.

Others have made history at Daytona too. Danica Patrick became the first female driver to win the pole position at a NASCAR Sprint Cup race there in 2013. She is among NASCAR's most popular drivers. The sport's most popular driver remains Dale Earnhardt Jr. In 2013 he was awarded that title by NASCAR for the eleventh straight year. Upon accepting his award after the 2013 season, Earnhardt said: "It humbles me deeply to know that you have so many fans in your corner each race weekend."

chapter 2

RACING'S ROOTS RUN DEEP

NASCAR exists because of Bill France Sr. He was a forceful man. Many knew him simply as "Big Bill" because he stood 6 feet 5 inches tall. France had a passion for auto racing. He saw a need to better organize the sport in the 1940s. France gathered about three dozen racers in a hotel in Daytona Beach, Florida, in 1947 to create a new

Bill France Sr. became a legend in stock car racing after he helped create NASCAR in 1947.

Darlington Raceway in South Carolina, shown hosting the Southern 500 in 1957, was the site of the first NASCAR race on a paved track.

racing series. NASCAR was born. NASCAR stands for National Association for Stock Car Auto Racing.

The sport's first "Strictly Stock" race was held with 33 cars in 1949 at Charlotte Fairgrounds Speedway in North Carolina. Glenn Dunnaway crossed the finish line first, but he is not listed as the winner. NASCAR saw that the rear springs in Dunnaway's car had been altered. That was against the rules.

NASCAR took the win from Dunnaway. Jim Roper, who had finished second, was declared the winner.

Lee Petty quickly became NASCAR's most successful driver. He also was the first driver to win three series championships. His son, Richard, later passed him in both categories.

As the years progressed, so did the sport. NASCAR's first race on a paved track was in 1950 at Darlington Raceway in South Carolina. That race was the Southern 500. It also was the first 500-mile (805 km) race in the sport's history.

The first Daytona 500 was held in 1959 at Daytona International Speedway. The finish was so close that the winner was not declared until three days later. Officials found a picture that showed Lee Petty nipping Johnny Beauchamp for the victory.

NASCAR's First Family

The France family has played an important role in NASCAR history. Bill France Sr. is the father of NASCAR. His son, Bill France Jr., took over as NASCAR chairman in 1972. Bill France Jr. then stepped aside to allow his son, Brian, to lead NASCAR in 2003.

Daytona also provided one of the sport's biggest moments in 1979. That was the first year TV network CBS showed the Daytona 500 live on TV from start to finish. A blizzard covered most of the East Coast of the United States with snow. That kept people at home. Many tuned in to the race. They saw an exciting finish.

Donnie Allison and Cale Yarborough battled for the lead on the final lap. Yarborough was second. He tried to pass Allison on the backstretch to take the lead. Allison blocked him. They bumped twice and then crashed in Turn 3. Richard Petty zipped past them to win the race.

Team Effort

NASCAR teams have grown through the years. Some teams have several buildings on what they call a "campus." Many teams build their own cars. Some build their own engines. Many top teams have around 500 people working for them.

Teams need many mechanics to help build and take care of the cars. A big team likely will have a dozen or more different cars available to run during the season. They need so many cars because there are many different types of tracks. Teams also need pit crew members at the track on race day to service the car during pit stops.

The costs of running a team are high. Team officials work with businesses and other sponsors to bring in millions of dollars. Teams could not survive without that money.

Cale Yarborough, *right*, fought with Bobby Allison, *center*, and brother Donnie Allison after a crash at the 1979 Daytona 500.

Attention soon turned back to Turn 3. Bobby Allison stopped to make sure his brother Donnie was OK. Yarborough approached. He was upset with Bobby Allison for an earlier incident. Bobby Allison and Yarborough argued. Yarborough then punched Bobby Allison. Soon they were fighting. That fight and finish helped the sport gain attention and grow.

The pit crew is just one part of a NASCAR team that works to help make a driver successful on race day.

Another major moment came in 1992 at the Atlanta Motor Speedway. It was the last race of the year. It marked the final race for Richard Petty, who was retiring. Six drivers entered the race with a chance at the season championship. Alan Kulwicki nipped Bill Elliott for the checkered flag in one of the closer battles for the title. Fans celebrated Kulwicki's victory while they waved good-bye to Petty.

Another important event happened in 2001 at Daytona. It marked the first year of NASCAR's TV agreement with networks FOX and NBC. That deal allowed more people to watch NASCAR races. The 2001 Daytona 500 also is remembered for a last-lap crash that involved Dale Earnhardt Sr., one of the greatest drivers of all time. Earnhardt died from the injuries suffered in that crash. His death led to NASCAR adopting a new restraint system to protect drivers.

The following year was Jimmie Johnson's rookie season. He would go on to win six series championships by 2013, including five in a row. Many already consider him one of the best drivers in NASCAR history, even though his career is still young.

chapter 3

STOCK CARS TO MAGNIFICENT MACHINES

Imagine going to a racetrack and watching a race between the type of cars you see on the street. It was possible years ago. The first cars that raced in NASCAR could be driven on the street. In those days, some people rigged their cars to go fast because they hauled homemade alcohol, called moonshine, on the road. That was illegal. If the police caught them with moonshine,

Cars turn a corner at Daytona's famous Beach Road course in a 1954 race.

they could go to jail. So the drivers had fast cars to help them avoid the police. Many of those men went on to race those cars, and NASCAR was born.

Numbers Game

NASCAR race cars are often colorful and feature numerous sponsor logos from bumper to bumper. But most fans remember drivers by their car's number. Richard Petty made the No. 43 famous. The team he co-owns continues to run that number. Dale Earnhardt Sr. made the No. 3 famous. No driver in the Sprint Cup Series used No. 3 until 2014, when Austin Dillon debuted in the No. 3 car. Dillon is the grandson of Richard Childress, who was Earnhardt's best friend and team owner of Richard Childress Racing.

The cars that raced in NASCAR's early years could be bought from a car dealership. They needed only minor changes to get them ready to race. The headlights were taped over. The muffler was removed. Seat belts were required. The doors had to be strapped or bolted shut. The cars also had to have strong rear axles to keep the cars from flipping.

Those cars marked the first generation of NASCAR racers in

what is now the Sprint Cup Series. The second-generation race car ran from 1967 to 1980. Teams were allowed to modify the car's frame. They also began to focus on aerodynamics in the 1970s. An aerodynamic vehicle cuts through the air with less resistance. That helps it go faster. The Dodge Daytona car improved its aerodynamics with a tall rear wing.

One of the biggest changes to the car during this time was adding a window net on the driver's side. That happened after Richard Petty's accident in 1970 at Darlington Raceway. His car flipped several times. Petty's left arm and shoulder were injured because they hung outside the car as it tumbled. The netting keeps a driver's arm and shoulder inside the car in a crash.

NASCAR changed its cars again in 1981. Car manufacturers began making smaller cars. NASCAR vehicles got smaller too. Technology helped make the cars go faster. Bill Elliott set a qualifying record of 212.809 mph (342.483 km/h) in 1987 at Talladega Superspeedway.

Bobby Allison survived this wreck in 1976, but crashes like this one showed NASCAR officials the need for better safety measures to protect drivers.

That extra speed was fine if the cars ran without problems. But if a car got into trouble, a driver could lose control quickly. A tire blew on Bobby Allison's car in 1987 at Talladega. His car slid and became airborne. It crashed into the fence that protects the fans.

NASCAR officials decided they needed to slow the cars. They required a restrictor plate at some tracks. A restrictor plate is a thin metal plate with four holes in it. It limits how much air gets into the engine. That reduces the engine's horsepower. Restrictor plates remained a part of NASCAR in 2014.

The fourth generation of race car was used from 1992 to 2006. Teams were allowed more freedom to modify the car's body. Teams spent hours testing the cars in wind tunnels trying to find ways to make the cars faster. A wind tunnel moves air around a car to simulate racing conditions.

The fifth generation of race car was used from 2007 to 2012. The cars featured safety improvements to help protect the driver in an accident. All the cars were similar, even if they were built by Dodge, Toyota, Chevrolet, or Ford. They also added a rear wing. Many fans did not like how that looked. NASCAR later replaced the wing with a spoiler.

That led to the current type of race car. It is called the Gen-6 because it is the sixth generation of race car. This car is fast. It set qualifying records for 19 races in 2013. It also

Brad Keselowski drives the new Gen-6 car at Daytona International Speedway in 2013.

provides more protection for the drivers. Engineers made the roll cage stronger. They also added larger roof flaps to limit the chances of the car flying into the air in a crash.

Another key change is that the Gen-6 cars look more like cars that are on the road. That is important for the manufacturers that want to advertise and sell their cars. The Gen-6 car helps keep their companies in business.

NASCAR Photo Diagram

1. **RADIATOR AIR INTAKE:** This directs air into the radiator to help cool engine fluids.

2. **HOOD PINS:** Four metal pins with tethers keep the hood closed.

3. **TIRES:** Radial tires are designed for racing only.

4. **DRIVER'S NAME:** The driver's last name is placed at the top of the windshield to help fans identify each car.

5. **WINDOW NET:** This safety device keeps a driver's head and arms inside the car during an accident.

6. **JACK POST:** This marks the spot for the pit crew to place the jack that lifts the car during pit stops.

7. **REAR SPOILER:** This directs the air over the rear of the car to provide downforce, which helps make the car easier to handle.

chapter 4

SUPER SKILLS

Jeff Gordon began racing when he was five years old. Tony Stewart first drove a go-kart at age five. Jimmie Johnson started racing motocross at age five. They are among NASCAR's best drivers. While age five is not a magic number for racers, they all succeeded with an early start in racing. The more they raced, the more experience they gained. That helped make them better drivers.

Many drivers have since followed them by starting early. Some drivers reached

Jeff Gordon, *right*, shown with Dale Earnhardt Sr., raced for years before making his debut on the NASCAR circuit.

Learning the Ropes

Drivers work their way up to the NASCAR Sprint Cup Series. Some compete in the Camping World Truck Series. Teams race modified pickup trucks on many of the same tracks used in the Sprint Cup Series.

Many drivers move from the Truck Series to the Nationwide Series. Cars used in the Nationwide Series have less horsepower than cars in the Sprint Cup Series. The Nationwide Series provides a good training ground for drivers. Many of NASCAR's top drivers raced in the Nationwide Series before moving to the Sprint Cup Series.

NASCAR's top series before they turned 20. Joey Logano made his NASCAR Sprint Cup debut at age 18 in 2008.

Good drivers need excellent eyesight and quick reflexes. A car traveling 170 mph (274 km/h) travels the length of a football field in a little more than one second. Excellent eyesight and quick reflexes help a driver avoid accidents at high speeds.

But it takes more than that. Drivers have to be in good physical shape because of the conditions in which they race. The temperature inside a car can reach 130 degrees Fahrenheit (54 degrees Celsius).

Some sports fans have questioned whether NASCAR drivers are athletes. In 2013 Donovan McNabb, a former

The Camping World Truck Series gives young drivers a chance to show their skills while they prepare to drive on the NASCAR circuit.

professional football player, said that Johnson was not an athlete because Johnson only sat in a car. But Johnson's regular training routine includes swimming, running, and biking. Late in 2013, he was running approximately 30 to 40 miles (48 to 64 km) per week. He also has biked 100 miles (161 km) per week at times.

Many drivers work out to stay in shape for their races. Proper conditioning keeps them from getting tired in the car.

A tired driver is more likely to make mistakes. Drivers often lift weights and run. Some drivers have run in half-marathon races. That is where they run 13.1 miles (21.1 km).

Driving in a NASCAR race can be as grueling as running a half-marathon. A 2012 ESPN *Sports Science* study found that Denny Hamlin lost 13 pounds (5.9 kilograms) in water weight from sweating during a 600-mile (966 km) race. He lost that weight while driving his car for about four hours. The report also stated that Hamlin's sustained heart rate was 130 beats a minute during the race. That is the same as an elite endurance runner.

The best NASCAR drivers also have to spend a lot of time studying. They watch videos of a previous race at the track where they are going to compete. That helps remind them of some of the tricky conditions they might face at that track.

Drivers also keep notes on how the car handled on a track. They study those notes like they are preparing for a test. If a

NASCAR teams often represent multiple sponsors that help fund their efforts on the track.

driver cannot tell his team what the car is doing, they cannot make the right changes to help the car run faster.

Another important skill is one that is often overlooked. Drivers represent their sponsors. Drivers need to speak well in interviews and act responsibly on and off the track. Sponsors will find another driver if one of their drivers does not represent them well.

Some sponsors pay millions of dollars to have their name or logo on a stock car. That money helps fund the race team. In 2012 the Army National Guard had a budget of $26.5 million for its NASCAR program. That included sponsorship of Dale Earnhardt Jr.'s car.

Racing is one sport where men and women can compete against each other. Danica Patrick completed her first full season in the Sprint Cup Series in 2013. She was the fastest qualifier for the Daytona 500 in 2013, which earned her the pole position.

Patrick is not the only female to drive in NASCAR's national series. Johanna Long regularly competed in the Nationwide Series in 2013. That series is a step below the Sprint Cup Series. Long and Patrick showed that women can be as fast as men racing cars.

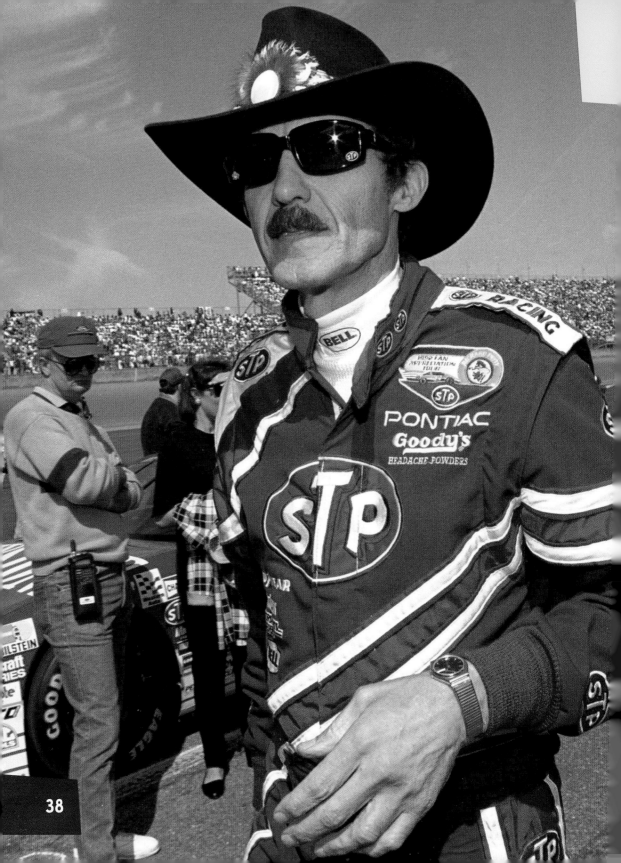

chapter 5

THE KING AND HIS COURT

H is name is Richard Petty, but he is better known as "The King." Petty is considered one of the greatest NASCAR drivers ever. His 200 victories are more than any other driver. He won seven championships. He also won the Daytona 500 a record seven times.

Petty is known as The King for more than his success on the track. He is also famous for his kindness. Many fans tell stories of Petty staying well after he raced until every

Richard Petty is known as "The King," in part because he won more NASCAR races than any driver in history.

fan who wanted his autograph got one. He raced from 1958 to 1992. He remains a part of the sport since his retirement. Petty wearing his trademark sunglasses and cowboy hat is a common sight at the track.

The only driver who matched Petty with seven championships was Dale Earnhardt Sr. He was known as "The Intimidator." He drove a black No. 3 car for most of his career. Earnhardt was not afraid to bump drivers out of the way if needed. That made him intimidating. Many fans liked him for his aggressive style and for all the races he won.

Earnhardt died from injuries suffered in a crash during the 2001 Daytona 500. He and Petty both were selected for the first class of the NASCAR Hall of Fame.

Minority Trailblazers

Wendell Scott is the only black driver to have won a race in NASCAR's top division. He won the Jacksonville 200 in 1963. Darrell Wallace Jr. became the first black driver to win a national NASCAR race since Scott. Wallace won a Camping World Truck Series race in 2013 at Martinsville Speedway.

Some might argue that David Pearson was the greatest driver in NASCAR history. Even Richard Petty said Pearson was the best there has ever been. Pearson won 105 races. That was better than every other driver except Petty. Pearson also won three championships. He was known as "The Silver Fox." He got that nickname because of his gray hair and because he was smart like a fox. Pearson did not always run at the front during the first part of the race. But on the final lap, Pearson was usually near the front.

Jimmie Johnson is also considered among the best drivers in the sport's history. He won his sixth Sprint Cup championship in 2013. That put him just one championship behind Richard Petty and Dale Earnhardt Sr. Johnson won five consecutive titles from 2006 to 2010. Nobody had ever won more than three championships in a row until Johnson's streak.

Jimmie Johnson has become one of the most dominant drivers in the modern era of NASCAR.

Jeff Gordon is one of Johnson's Hendrick Motorsports teammates. Gordon has won four championships through 2013. He was the first driver to win the Brickyard 400 at Indianapolis Motor Speedway four times.

Other big winners include Hall of Famers Darrell Waltrip, Bobby Allison, and Cale Yarborough. Waltrip won three championships and 84 Sprint Cup races. Allison won one title and 84 races. Yarborough won three championships and 83 races.

Waltrip won a record 12 races, including seven in a row, at Bristol Motor Speedway between 1978 and 1992. After he retired, he became a broadcaster for FOX Sports. Yarborough won four Daytona 500s. Only Richard Petty won it more often. Allison's most famous victory came in the 1988 Daytona 500. It was his third Daytona 500 win. His son, Davey, finished second in that race. It was the first time in the race's history that a father and son had finished in the top two.

Johnson and Gordon have some tough competition in the current era of NASCAR. Tony Stewart has won three championships and is considered one of the more talented drivers in this era. Brad Keselowski won the championship in 2012. Matt Kenseth has also won a championship.

GLOSSARY

AERODYNAMICS

How air flowing around a car can affect its speed and handling.

CAUTION PERIOD

A time when drivers must slow down because the track has become unsafe due to an accident, debris, or bad weather.

CHECKERED FLAG

A flag of black and white squares waved when the winner crosses the finish line.

HORSEPOWER

A measurement of engine power equal to the amount of power it takes to move 33,000 pounds (14,969 kg) 1 foot (30 cm) in a minute.

POLE POSITION

The first car in line at the start of a race.

RESTRICTOR PLATE

A thin metal plate with four holes that restricts airflow from the carburetor into the engine. This reduces horsepower and keeps speeds down.

ROOKIE

A first-year driver in a series.

SAFETY TRUCK

A pickup truck equipped with safety equipment that goes to the scene of an accident during a race and helps the driver.

SPOILER

A metal blade attached to the back of the car. It helps restrict airflow over the rear of the car, helping make it more aerodynamic.

FOR MORE INFORMATION

Further Readings

Blount, Terry. *The Blount Report: NASCAR's Most Overrated & Underrated Drivers, Cars, Teams, and Tracks*. Chicago IL: Triumph Books, 2009.

Canfield, Jack, Mark Victor Hansen, and Cathy Elliott. *Chicken Soup for the Soul NASCAR: 101 Stories of Family, Fortitude and Fast Cars*. Deerfield Beach, FL: Health Communications, 2003.

Edelstein, Robert. *NASCAR Legends: Memorable Men, Moments, and Machines in Racing History*. New York: The Overlook Press, 2011.

Hembree, Mike. *"Then Tony Said to Junior ..." The Best NASCAR Stories Ever Told*. Chicago IL: Triumph Books, 2009.

Long, Dustin. *The Daytona 500*. Minneapolis, MN: Abdo Publishing Company, 2013.

Websites

To learn more about Inside the Speedway, visit **booklinks.abdopublishing.com**. These links are routinely monitored and updated to provide the most current information available.

INDEX

Allison, Bobby, 17, 25, 45
Allison, Davey, 45
Allison, Donnie, 16–17
Atlanta Motor Speedway, 18

Beauchamp, Johnny, 15
Brickyard 400, 44
Bristol Motor Speedway, 45

Camping World Truck Series, 32, 40
Charlotte Fairgrounds Speedway, 14
Childress, Richard, 22

Darlington Raceway, 15, 24
Daytona 500, 5–6, 8–9, 15–17, 19, 37, 39, 40, 45
Daytona International Speedway, 5–6, 15
Dillon, Austin, 22
Dunnaway, Glenn, 14–15

Earnhardt, Dale, Jr., 10, 37
Earnhardt, Dale, Sr., 8, 9, 19, 22, 40, 43
Elliott, Bill, 19, 24
engines, 16, 26

France, Bill, Jr., 15
France, Bill, Sr., 13, 15
France, Brian, 15

Gordon, Jeff, 31, 44, 45

Hamlin, Denny, 34
Hendrick Motorsports, 44

Indianapolis Motor Speedway, 44

Johnson, Jimmie, 9, 10, 19, 31, 33, 43–45

Kenseth, Matt, 45
Keselowski, Brad, 45
Kulwicki, Alan, 18–19

Logano, Joey, 32
Long, Johanna, 37

Martinsville Speedway, 40
McNabb, Donovan, 32
Montoya, Juan Pablo, 5–6

Nationwide Series, 32, 37

Patrick, Danica, 10, 37
Pearson, David, 43

Petty, Lee, 15
Petty, Richard, 9–10, 15, 16, 18–19, 22, 24, 39–40, 43, 45

Reagan, Ronald, 10
Roper, Jim, 15

safety measures, 6, 8, 25–26
Scott, Wendell, 40
Southern 500, 15
Sprint Cup Series, 8, 9, 10, 22, 24, 32, 37, 43, 45
Stewart, Tony, 31, 45

Talladega Superspeedway, 24, 25

Wallace, Darrell Jr., 40
Waltrip, Darrell, 5–6, 45

Yarborough, Cale, 16–17, 45

About the Author

Dustin Long is an award-winning journalist who is the senior writer at Motor Racing Network (MRN.com). His work has appeared in *USA Today*, *The New York Times*, and SI.com. In 2011 he won the George Cunningham Writer of the Year Award for his NASCAR coverage. Raised in Indiana, he lives near Charlotte, North Carolina, with his wife.